THE
FISHERMAN

Leadership Traits to
Win the Game of Life

DAVE STECKEL
WITH
JASON THOMAS

THE FISHERMAN

Published by Cross Training Publishing

Printed and Distributed by Cross Training Publishing

15418 Weir Street #177

Omaha, NE 68137 U.S.A.

Dave Steckel

www.crosstrainingpublishing.com

308-293-3891

Paperback ISBN 978-1-938254-85-7

Printed in the United States of America

First Edition 2019

To MaryBeth and Amanda
All these years of patience, understanding, and love.
As Jackie Gleason said on The Honeymooner's,
You're the greatest.

CONTENTS

FOREWORD

When I'm asked what makes a great leader, one of the key characteristics I always share is that they care. And that's what I love about Coach Stec. He cares. He cares about his team. He cares about his players. He cares about his university. He cares about his community. Most importantly he cares about his family. Coach Stec is a leader who cares about others, and it's why he is a difference maker on and off the field.

In this book, Coach Stec's care for others and his desire to develop future leaders is very evident. Combining his military service and coaching experience he shares many valuable insights to help readers become better leaders. Through his in-depth but lively dialogue with the Fisherman's character (who has an extensive Marine background), Coach Stec shows how the same great leadership qualities apply to the military, sports and everyday life.

Coach Stec has spent his life working to make the people around him better, and I believe reading his book will make you better as well. We can all grow in our leadership and Coach Stec provides a story and powerful, practical insights to make this growth possible.

-Jon Gordon, best-selling author of *The Energy Bus* and *The Carpenter*.

ACKNOWLEDGEMENTS

Football games can NOT be won without the contributions of your teammates. The same is true with the game of life.

You need many people to help you be successful. Same goes for this book. Huge thank you to Jason Thomas who took my thoughts and words and described an incredible story to match the perfect leadership qualities. Couldn't do it without you Bro! To MaryBeth, my wife, for her proofreading and grammar critique. Thank you to Lynn Mentzer, who helped type my handwriting and email Jason. Appreciate you Lynn. A big thank you to Nancy Allen, a law professor at Missouri State and NY Times Best Selling Author. I really appreciate your time and guidance on getting this book published. A sincere thank you to Chad Bonham. Appreciate you listening to me and coordinating my talk with Gordon Thiessen. And Gordon, thank you for making this all a reality. To Jon Gordon... Appreciate your support and encouragement for me getting to write this book. Thank you.

And a huge thank you to the Good Lord for all the experiences and relationships the game of football gave me and my family.

Proverbs 3:5

CHAPTER ONE

Casting a Line

The fisherman baits the J-hook with a peeled grass shrimp, arches his rod from his front to his back like a catapult, and flicks the fishing line into the Atlantic Ocean.

From his spot at the end of the pier he squints as the foamy waves carry the line back toward shore, the long-dead bait having disappeared into the depths. His thoughts drift to something his commanding officer told him more than six decades ago, not long before the fisherman would make Marine Corps history.

"The ocean has no memory."

The line drifts with the tide.

"Still have no idea what that means," the fisherman says to a few gulls pecking at worms squirming in the fading sun. He removes his Montford Point Marine Association hat and scratches his bald head.

"But I sure did make a lot of memories."

The gulls never look up.

A tug on his line jolts the fisherman back to his purpose; hook some fish.

I trudge through the sand toward the pier, oblivious to the setting sun melting into the ocean, shrouding the beach in a haze of cranberry and purple.

Before me is a painting, the kind that lulls you into a trance, like that in-between world when you're drifting off to sleep—half of your mind entering a dream, the other still hard-wired to reality.

My thoughts—on our next season, the Xs and Os, diagrams in black and white, a stark contrast to the scene right before my eyes—drill a hole into my mind.

I barely notice the old man stumbling down the last step of

the pier, struggling to keep a grip on his fishing rod and basket. The Marine eagle, globe and anchor on his hat glint in the fading light.

"Semper Fi," I say, one Marine to another, my calves aching as I hurry my pace to help the fisherman.

"Oorah!" the old man says, straightening himself as best he can.

"Stec," I say, jutting out my hand.

"They call me The Fisherman," he says, gripping my hand with a strength that jars me back to reality.

"What kind of name is The Fisherman?"

"What kind of name is Stec?"

I like him from the start.

CHAPTER TWO

The Dream

That night I have a dream.

I'm at Marine Boot Camp on Parris Island.

"Everyone, on the bus!" the drill sergeant barks at our whole battalion, which is standing at attention in a driving rainstorm in the dead of night.

After what seems like a five-second ride—the only thing I can glimpse by looking out the window is an ENTERING MONTFORD POINT CAMP sign—we are ordered off the bus in the same manner as we are told to get on—sternly.

Each company of the battalion is told to fall in, and wait, the rain pelting our faces stings like sand on a wind-blown beach.

"Ears?" the drill instructor barks.

"Open, sir!" we scream back.

"Eyeballs?" he yells.

"Click, sir!" we shout back.

"Parade rest."

Like a flock of starling in olive drab, my company shifts the weight of their left feet exactly twelve inches to the left of their right feet in one fluid motion. At the same time we clasp our hands below our belt at the small of our backs, right hand inside left hand.

While at ease I notice a company drilling in the distance. I crane my neck slightly and squint for a better look. No one else in my company seems to notice the all-black recruits.

"About, face!" their drill instructor barks. The company slides their right feet behind their left and spins 180 degrees with the precision and grace of a dance troupe. Their arms never move.

"Forward, march!" the officer screams. The company lurches forward in unison.

As the recruits pass nearby my eyes meet with the drill instructor's. Just as he gives a slight nod a flash of lightning illuminates the Marines eagle, globe and anchor on his hat and the words "Montford Point Marine Association."

Where have I seen those words? Where have I seen this man?

The pelting rain feels all too real on my face. The recruits, and the drill instructor, fade into the darkness.

CHAPTER THREE

Passion

I awake to a bright and beautiful morning. Liquid gold on a beach vacation.

My usual walk on the beach is made more difficult by sand thick from an overnight rain.

Suddenly I remember last night's dream. The rain. The drill instructor.

Gulls squawking over a half-eaten bagel snap me out of my trance.

As I near the pier where I met The Fisherman yesterday I keep my eyes peeled to see if he is at it again. The silhouette casting a line into the water is unmistakably his.

He catches a glimpse of me approaching, and to my surprise, waves me up. I make my way along the wet wood planks to where The Fisherman stands, staring at his line drifting toward shore. I wonder how many times he's performed this ritual.

"Anything biting?" I say as I rest my elbow on the pier's railing, asking the fisherman the only question that I, a non-fisherman, can think of.

"A little fish called Moby Dick," the old man says with a chuckle. "You know, a fisherman never tells anyone if anything is biting. He might as well tell you the secret to life."

"Which is?"

"Never go grocery shopping on an empty stomach."

We both laugh. As The Fisherman smiles I notice a scar on the left side of his face that runs from his temple to his lower jaw.

"How about I ask the questions today?" The Fisherman says.

The tone of his voice commands with authority. Almost like I'm in boot camp again.

"Shoot," I tell The Fisherman.

"What's your passion?"

His question catches me off guard. I feel myself recoil a bit. I figure the old man wants to know what I do for a living. I usually hate telling people that I'm a college football coach. The conversation typically turns to sports. Everyone has an opinion about sports—and I couldn't care less about anyone's opinion about sports.

The Fisherman is different, though. He seems more immersed in his task of reeling in fish than talking about sports.

"Coaching," I say, answering his question.

"What is it about coaching that makes it your passion?" he says in return, as he begins to reel in his line.

"The ability to impact young men's lives," I say, "and to help guide them in shaping their future."

"Interesting," The Fisherman says, hypnotically reeling in his line while never varying the speed of his hand. "Being a coach must require being a great leader. And being a leader means possessing certain qualities."

I realize The Fisherman is not concerned about offering an opinion about sports.

"That's right," I say half-heartedly, wondering what the old man knows about being a leader.

The Fisherman finishes reeling in his line. Nothing has clasped onto his bait, a mud minnow.

"I saw you noticed my scar," he says, turning to look at me.

I don't answer. Instead I shift my eyes to the endless ocean.

"Bayonet," the old man says. "Purple Heart Ridge near Mount Tapotchau, Saipan."

I feel like burying my head in the sand for having privately dissed The Fisherman's experience.

"You learn a lot about leadership when you stare down a stampede of thousands of madmen on a god-forsaken rock thousands of miles from home. You also learn who you can trust with your life. And you learn that deep down, each of us has the strength to move mountains."

The Fisherman takes the minnow off the hook and tosses it over the side of the pier.

"What I saw on the peak of that hill in the middle of nowhere informed me for the rest of my life."

He goes on to say that the qualities essential to being a leader will earn a person much in return, including: RESPECT, CONFIDENCE and the LOYAL COOPERATION of others.

"Once you find the meaning of each trait you can achieve your dreams and goals," the old man says, securing the hook at the end of his line onto a ring on his fishing rod.

The Fisherman probably notices my jaw scraping the pier after what he has just told me.

He puts his extra hooks and sinkers into his tackle box and snaps it shut. The Fisherman then straightens his Montford Point Marines hat.

"Better get a move on," he says, slapping my shoulder. "I'm sure you've got a busy day planned with your family."

CHAPTER FOUR
Judgment

Proverbs 2:6: "For the Lord gives wisdom,
from his mouth comes knowledge and understanding."

The Fisherman and I ease into a daily ritual—him casting his line into the ocean, never catching anything; me hanging on his every word.

On this day judgment is the topic of choice.

How often do we judge someone without first getting to know him? Maybe it's his looks, or what he's wearing—in our own mind we often instantly like or dislike someone solely based on outward appearance.

The same holds true for coaches, mostly based on a player's actions, we're always judging.

"As I coach I'm guilty of constantly judging my players," I say meekly.

But judging isn't what The Fisherman has in mind.

"I'm not talking about judging," he says, this time reclining in a camping chair that he brought with him to the pier. "I'm talking about judgment. Big difference. Judging is a verb ... leaders don't judge. Judgment is a noun—with knowledge and understanding you can make sound decisions."

This logic strikes a chord with me. I thank The Fisherman for our chat and walk off the pier and onto the beach to continue my stroll.

I think about starting as a graduate assistant, moving to an assistant coach, being elevated to a coordinator and now a head football coach and leading groups of different young men, and how I have to make sound judgments for them.

Along all those moves, decisions are always going to be

made; however, the thought of team is more important than individuals. In football many judgments are made on position changes, or depth-chart changes. Open and honest dialogue with the individual is always paramount for total understanding.

One of the toughest judgments that get made as far as "team" centers on discipline. When I first came to Missouri State we had an all-conference player who was our offensive center. He would not buy into the culture and our plan. After many conversations, we suspended him from our team. We asked him to come back with a great attitude, and he could be reinstated.

He never came back.

How are sound judgments accomplished? By being FAIR, CONSISTENT and DEMANDING— all-important aspects of leadership. At the same time it's critical not to judge the people you are in charge of, and more importantly, not to judge the people above you.

JUDGMENT

Know:

Judging is your ability to think clearly and calmly. To be fair, consistent and demanding on yourself and others. To consider all sides of a situation and base rewards and punishment, without delay in a professional manner. Using tact, while maintaining great relationships.

Improvements:

Avoid making rash decisions by using common sense. Be honest and avoid favoritism. Stay positive and treat people how you want to be treated.

CHAPTER FIVE

Unselfishness

Philippians 2:4: "Everyone should look out not only for his own interest, but also the interest of others."

"We're both Marines, right?" The Fisherman asks, beginning this day's conversation with a question.

"Through and through," I reply.

That prompts another question.

"What do you know about the history of the Marines? Specifically, black Marines?"

Despite the morning's chill I feel a cold sweat break out across my forehead. I never considered myself much of a student of anything, much less a student of history.

Before I can answer, The Fisherman speaks.

"Remember this name, Gilbert "Hashtag" Johnson," The Fisherman says, knotting his fishing line around the J-hook that holds today's bait—a fiddler crab. "Cool nickname, huh?"

We like nicknames.

"Hashtag had already served two stints totaling nine years in the Army and returned to civilian life before he decided to join the U.S. Navy, which was segregated at the time, where he served nine years," The Fisherman says while flicking his line into the ocean. "While he was serving aboard the U.S.S. Wyoming, President Roosevelt issued an executive order banning racial discrimination in the armed services."

"You know what Hashtag did when he heard that?"

The Fisherman can tell by the look on my face that I have no idea, because he answers for me.

"He immediately enlisted in the Marine Corps."

With a sense of pride, The Fisherman goes on to tell me how Hashtag became one of the first black drill sergeants in Marine Corps history. How when serving with a battalion in Guam and learning that black Marines were being assigned to labor details rather than combat patrols, he convinced his commanding officers to let them fight alongside their fellow Marines. And how Hashtag led more than 20 excursions into the thick jungle.

"You know why he did these things?" The Fisherman asks, watching the waves lap against his fishing line.

"Because he was unselfish," The Fisherman says, before I could utter a word.

"He knew he was part of something much greater than himself. That he'd shape the lives of and illuminate the path for the next generation. He was the very definition of a leader."

I was speechless. Then it hit me; there are few people in my life, other than my wife and daughter, who I enjoy spending time with in intimate conversations. The Fisherman quickly made that list.

"I'm reminded of a quote from a guy named Zig Ziglar," says The Fisherman, unwrapping a pimento cheese sandwich after having put down his fishing rod for a break.

Zig Ziglar? I tell The Fisherman I'm intimately aware of him and his books, and have in fact read them and keep them in my office. I was introduced to his books by legendary college football coach Lou Holtz while working with him at the University of Minnesota. Between bites of his sandwich The Fisherman delivers one of his favorite quotes by Ziglar:

"You get what you want when you really help others get what they want."

"Bite?" The Fisherman asks, waving his sandwich toward me.

"No thanks," I say with a laugh.

I thank The Fisherman for another great conversation and bid him a good day.

As I walk along the beach I think about when I was promoted to defensive coordinator at the University of Missouri. I could never have accomplished any success without the other assistant coaches and the valuable input they provided. These coaches—Cornell Ford, Craig Kuligowski, Alex Grinch and Barry Odom—provided me with insightful knowledge, friendship and immeasurable support in our goal as a defensive unit to become great. It was all about WE.

We were unselfish.

We paralleled having a great staff with having a great defense. We had great players who had fun, played together and understood the plan.

One game we picked off a pass and ran it back for a touchdown. On the video review we could see ten guys celebrating, and one guy walking off the field by himself. Coaches quickly had a meeting with this player and told him he would not play if he continued to be selfish and show low morale and disrespect for his team. That player, Shane Ray, reevaluated his priorities and became a great teammate and first round NFL draft pick.

He became unselfish.

UNSELFISHNESS

Know:

When you're unselfish you avoid making yourself comfortable at the expense of others. Give credit to others.

Improvements:

Avoid using your position for personal gain. Get out of yourself and get into the TEAM.

CHAPTER SIX

Initiative

Proverbs 10:4: "A lazy hand makes one poor,
but diligent hands bring riches."

Another day starts as a dreary, drizzly morning. It is summer at the beach, so I expect the mist should stop soon.

I am sitting on the porch drinking my coffee and my mind starts to wonder about The Fisherman, and if he will be out there on a day like today. It is pretty warm already, and there is a slight haze around the sun from the drizzle. I decide to take a walk and see if The Fisherman has the initiative to get up and cast his line on a day like today.

As I am walking on the beach, I see a lot of people not wanting to waste their limited vacation days sitting inside. I am surprised by this and hopeful The Fisherman likes to be out in this kind of weather too.

As I approach the pier I spot his unmistakable silhouette. He again waves me up to the pier.

"Wet enough for ya?" he says, his eyes peeking from underneath the hood of a forest green poncho.

"Bring it on!" I say with a smile. "I've coached in a helluva lot worse than this."

The Fisherman belts out a hearty laugh. The rain lightens and the old man peels back the poncho's hood.

"Saipan is located in what's known as Typhoon Alley," he says. "When I joined the Marines I knew I was wet behind the ears, but I never thought I'd literally be wet behind the ears in a foreign land in just a few short months. That's why I never leave home without one of these," he says, shedding his poncho now that the rain has let up and the sun has begun to peek out from behind the clouds.

"I could have used one of those on the sidelines many a time," I say.

The Fisherman smiles and begins his ritual of baiting his hook. This morning it's a shrimp.

"Remember our conversation about Hashtag Johnson yesterday?" he says, turning to look at me.

"Yes sir," I reply, wanting to prove myself as the attentive student.

The Fisherman goes on to talk about how a person must take action.

"When Gilbert Johnson transferred to the Marines, despite earning the rank of officer steward first class in the Navy—the equivalent to a Marine Corps gunnery sergeant—he had to give up both rank and pay. Yet he was so strong in his conviction that he never wavered. It took great initiative on his part to seize the opportunity to become a Marine.

"He went on to become one of the first black drill sergeants in Marine Corps history. Camp Montford Point, where black recruits attended boot camp before integration, would later be named Camp Johnson, in honor of Hashtag. More than 22,000 black Marines were trained at Camp Johnson, including yours truly."

Suddenly the dream I had the night after first meeting The Fisherman comes into focus. The all-black recruits. The drill sergeant. His Montford Point hat …

My mind begins to spin. It becomes difficult to distinguish a dream from reality. Is The Fisherman just a figment of my imagination?

A rumble of thunder—turns out the beach weather gods were going to have some fun on this day of vacation—coaxes my thoughts back to the pier.

"Have you ever read Matthew 25, verses 14-30?" The Fisherman asks.

"The one about the talents?" I ask.

"That's the one," he says.

He asks if I ever thought about the talents as personal traits and not just money. Thinking about it, I realize I never actually had. He tells me to go home, reread the passage and think about what he has just said. Homework typically makes me cringe, but I gladly accept this assignment.

"One last thing before you go," The Fisherman says.

He reaches down, grabs his poncho and hands it to me.

"Never know when a typhoon might come your way," he says with a wink.

At home, after reading the passage from Matthew I start thinking about my brother Les. Les was a scrappy guy from Pennsylvania who knew what he wanted and how to get it. After high school he hitchhiked across the country to Kansas to go to college. After college he joined the Marine Corps as an officer and enlisted during the Vietnam War. After his time was complete he decided to be a football coach.

He started his coaching career as a graduate assistant at the University of Colorado then was elevated to full time wide receiver coach. From there he went to the United States Naval Academy as a offensive line coach and then on to 24 years in the NFL. With many stops along the way, he acquired a lot of knowledge and has some great personal insights.

When I decided to become a college coach he offered words of advice—have the initiative to be the first one in the office and the last to leave. Do all of the jobs you are given, even the menial ones, with attention to detail and to the best of your ability.

My thoughts turn to the conversation I had with The Fisherman this morning about initiative.

I begin to drift off to sleep. A gentle thunder echoes in the distance.

INITIATIVE

Know:

Initiative means take action without specific orders, meeting new and unexpected situations with prompt action, and using resourcefulness to get something done without having complete methods available.

Improvements:

Work on staying mentally and physically alert. Understand things that need to be done and then do them without being told.

CHAPTER SEVEN

Courage

st Corinthians 13:16: "Be on guard, stand
rm in faith, be men of courage, be strong."

"See this?" The Fisherman asks, holding up a silver sardine. "To you and me," he says, sliding a hook through the sardine's belly, "it's just a tiny little fish. To something out there in the water, it represents life."

With a flick of his wrist The Fisherman sends the bait sailing, signaling the continuation of his daily ritual.

"Courage," The Fisherman mutters, almost inaudibly. "Courage ... does it take courage for something in that water to pluck a tiny sardine off a string? I guess wanting to stay alive is courageous in and of itself."

I start to open my mouth, not sure what I might say, when The Fisherman interrupts me.

"When we landed in Saipan we found the beach strung with barbed wire. Behind that, trenches slithered through the sand, with machine gun posts rising up every so often like cobras.

"They were ready for us."

The Fisherman removes his Montford Point Marines hat, dabs his brow with a handkerchief, and puts the hat back on.

"It was early morning. I remember lying on my back and looking up at the stars for what seemed like an eternity. It was probably no more than a few blinks of an eye. I thought about the other 799 Montford Point Marines spread across the same beach like stars scattered in the sky. All of us tossed into battle for the very first time."

Just then the old man snaps back his fishing rod, hoping a fish has taken his bait. Nothing.

"We started to advance up the beach when we heard a collective, piercing shrieking. The enemy was charging straight for us. It was an ungodly sight. We opened up our machine guns, gave it everything we had." The Fisherman reels in his line until it emerges from the water. The hook is picked clean. He grabs another sardine and starts to bait his hook.

"When it was over we assessed the casualties. I learned later that the first of us to die was Private Kenneth J. Tibbs. Cut down right there on the beach. He had a young girlfriend back home in Columbus, Ohio. He had a baby daughter he never got to meet." The Fisherman is about to cast his line into the ocean when he pauses and looks at me.

"That's courage."

He flicks his newly baited hook into the ocean.

"Stec, it takes courage not to give up five minutes before a miracle," he says. "Not long after Tibbs and many others gave their lives, we broke through the enemy line.

"Tibbs may not have been a lieutenant or a general, but he was a leader because he had courage," The Fisherman says, staring out at an everlasting ocean. "Any effective leader needs courage. Courage comes in many forms and in many experiences."

I thank him for his knowledge and walk on, thinking about my life as a coach. I ask myself, when have I encountered an example of courage?

I think back to the years I worked for Gary Pinkel, the winningest coach at The University of Toledo and The University of Missouri. He always said "Courage is doing the right thing. If you have to think about if it's right or wrong, it's probably wrong."

Coach Pinkel and the staff I was privileged to be a part

of took over a very poor team and had the courage to stick to and execute the plan. Even through adversity, disadvantages, hate mail (emails, texts and anonymous message board posts) we had a plan and saw it through.

Coach Pinkel had the courage to believe in and stand up for his assistant coaches and players and always had their back. He taught me as a head coach to praise in public and correct in private.

COURAGE

Know:

Courage allows you to remain calm while recognizing fear. Moral courage is for you to stand up for what is right, take responsibility when you are wrong. Physical courage means you can function effectively when you have pain and injury.

Improvements:

Practice self-discipline and focus. Force yourself out of your comfort zone until you are able to control reactions.

CHAPTER EIGHT

Endurance

Galatians 6:9: "Let us not grow weary of doing good for in due time we will reap, if we don't give up."

After a fitful night of sleep—a lot of tossing and turning as The Fisherman's lessons and thoughts of the upcoming football season swarm my subconscious—I decide to sleep in.

By 7 a.m. I tire of battling my own brain so I get up and start my day. Thinking music might put my mind at ease, I turn on my phone, but before I open my music app, I check my email. The last message I read is still open, a YouTube video from a college buddy. It's a clip of Bruce Springsteen performing "Thunder Road" live.

"Exactly what I need," I say out loud as I press play and let The Boss take over my brain. I sing at the top of my lungs to "Thunder Road" while readying for my daily stroll.

"Stec!" a voice comes from another room.

"What?" I answer, my mood rising with Springsteen's voice.

"Don't quit your day job!" the voice replies.

Leave it up to your family to keep you in check.

As I near the pier and our usual meeting spot I hear a familiar voice: Bruce Springsteen and a god-awful screech accompanying the lyrics.

Just like I was a few minutes ago, The Fisherman is singing along to The Boss. I know the song well, "No Surrender," released in 1984 on Bruce's "Born in the USA" album.

The Fisherman sees me walking down the pier and quickly shuts off his CD player.

"Hey, Fisherman," I say. "Don't quit your day job."

"Luckily," he quickly retorts, "I don't have one."

We both laugh.

"I love that song," The Fisherman says, fumbling around in his tackle box. "It's a reminder to keep moving forward, have endurance and succeed. You need to have the consistency of waking up and attacking the day, every day."

"Well said," I respond, explaining to the old man that we both have something in common as Bruce Springsteen fans.

"I knew I liked you for a reason," he says, this time opting for fake bait, a white bucktail, before zipping his line into the ocean.

"Going back to that Springsteen song," The Fisherman says, "no surrender is what kept the dream alive for countless successful companies."

"You ever hear of Dyson vacuums?" he asks.

I nod my head.

"It took Sir James Dyson 15 years and every penny to his name to create a workable bagless vacuum," The Fisherman says. "He developed more than 5,000 prototypes before finding one that worked. "This happens time and time again," The Fisherman says, reeling in his line with a fluid, rhythmic motion. "There are very few overnight successes. It all depends on an individual's belief in a dream and the endurance to bring a vision to fruition."

The Fisherman turns to look at me.

"The same could be said for any athletic team, I suppose," he says. "You can't turn a team around on belief alone. You have to have patience, fortitude, belief and most importantly, endurance. It takes a strong work ethic from the coaches and the players to make a team a winner."

I tell The Fisherman I can certainly relate to that.

My first lesson in endurance was joining the Marine Corps

out of high school. I was a cocky 18-year-old know-it-all. It didn't take me long to realize this was serious and I was training for battle.

This had been my first experience with "no retreat, no surrender." If I could survive boot camp and three years in the Marine Corps, I could survive a bunch of 18-year-old college kids, know-it-all fans and unsupportive administrations.

This leads me to tell The Fisherman about my stint as an assistant coach at Dickinson College in Carlisle, Pennsylvania. It was my first full-time job, at a small division three, highly academic college. Most of the kids were way smarter than me, but they had a strong work ethic and a love for the game. Those kids would never become professional football players, but mostly doctors, lawyers or extremely successful businessmen.

The team had been 0-and-forever, but the new coach they hired, Ed Sweeney, was like the Energizer Bunny; he just kept going and going, doing whatever it took to turn this team around. Within two years we were 7-3 and won the conference.

Talk about endurance and fortitude—the staff Sweens put together and the kids we recruited were all on the same page and worked toward the same goal. We weren't just a team; we were family. This team started the longest winning streak in the history of Dickinson College football. I am forever grateful for the lessons Ed taught me as a young coach and the skills and characteristics of endurance he taught me to use as a head coach today.

"Sounds like endurance is well-ingrained in you," The Fisherman says, after having patiently listened to me talk.

"Certainly is," I say.

I bid him a good day as I turn to continue my stroll along the beach.

"One more thing," I say, as I turn back and point at The Fisherman's CD player. "Don't quit your day job."

The old man lets out a hearty chuckle and keeps reeling in his line.

ENDURANCE

Know:

Endurance is the mental and physical stamina to withstand pain, fatigue, stress and hardship through condition and performance.

Improvements:

Strengthen your mind and body. Force your mind and body to finish all tasks when fatigue sets in.

CHAPTER NINE

Sunday Nap

After six days of walking and talking with The Fisherman, my thoughts are constantly on leadership. How can I, our coaches and more importantly, our players, become better leaders?

The Fisherman has me hooked on getting the best out of everyone involved in my program. Starting off day seven on my usual walk along the beach, I have a new perspective on the fundamental attributes that can help our team get better.

I start to think more about sacrifice and The Fisherman's retelling of the selflessness of those Marines storming the beach in Saipan. Guys like Kenneth J. Tibbs, whose life would be cut short before he even got a chance to meet his baby daughter.

What must go through your mind as your sacrifice your own life so others may live in freedom?

Football is just a game, but lessons are found within that can shape future leaders. God-willing, people like Tibbs.

Lost in my own thoughts I realize the pier is in front of me.

The Fisherman is nowhere in sight. Then it dawns on me, it's Sunday. Let the old Marine rest his bones, I think to myself.

I take a few steps so that I'm directly under the pier, looking out toward the ocean. I sit and recline in the sand. Massive pillars that support the structure on either side yawn into the distance, creating a tunnel that ends in a square—bringing a patch of the ocean's vast expanse into sharp focus.

I don't realize it then, but at the moment, everything crystal-lizes—The Fisherman's lessons, my own experiences, the sacrifices of others—into what will become a foundation for true leadership. Like the ocean through that square at the end of the pier, everything is coming into focus.

Judgment: Make sound decision.

Be: Unselfish

Show: Initiative

Have: Courage

And: Endure not just the journey of football, but life.

I close my eyes. I repeat the first letter of each of those traits over and over: J.U.I.C.E.

The crashing of the waves lulls me to sleep.

CHAPTER TEN

50 Yard Line

"Stec, ol' boy, wake up!" The Fisherman's voice booms overhead. "Early worm gets the fish!"

I brush the sand from my arms and hands and hop up and down to get it off my shorts.

"I sure hope your touchdown dance was better than that," The Fisherman says, chuckling, as he turns to walk up the steps of the pier.

"I was an offensive center," I reply, shaking the sand from my hair. "I couldn't sniff the end zone if you wrapped it in prime rib."

"Probably just too slow," The Fisherman says over his shoulder. "Fish is better for you anyway."

"Yeah, yeah," I say with a smile as I lumber up the pier's steps.

As I watch The Fisherman go through his ritual, I have an overwhelming sense of gratitude toward the man. Thankful that a complete stranger would take an interest in a kid from Whitehall, Pennsylvania—a kid with a passion for a sport that he would turn into a career. A good career that has spanned 30 years. But a career that has been missing something.

The Fisherman senses the way I'm looking at him, my pensive stare.

"Last time you had that look you were probably in math class at Kutztown," The Fisherman says with his trademark laugh.

"How did you know…?"

"Where you went to college?" The Fisherman finishes my thought.

"Man, just because I'm old doesn't mean I don't know how to use the internet," he says.

"What's on your mind?"

"My mind?" I stammer, my eyes now fixed on the end of the pier. "Oh. I was just thinking."

"About what?"

"How much you've taught me."

"How much I've taught you?" The Fisherman shoots back while slowly standing up, his bait in his hands. He locks eyes with me.

"Stec, we're only at the 50-yard line."

The words hang over me like a mist. My eyes drift again to the end of the pier. I feel like I'm sinking and floating, all at the same time.

A child shrieks in laughter nearby.

I startle awake. I'm underneath the pier. The two columns of pillars stretch out in front of me and come together at the end of the pier, almost like an arrow.

I stand up, brush the sand off my arms and legs, and hop up and down to shake the sand off my shorts.

Touchdown dance.

Suddenly I remember the conversation I just had with The Fisherman. I bound up the steps of the pier. A few gulls peck at tiny mollusks stuck between cracks of wooden planks. Turning my head I see some families trying their best at pier fishing with little luck.

The Fisherman is nowhere in sight.

Sunday, I say to myself. It was just a dream. Let the old man rest.

CHAPTER ELEVEN

Bearing

Matthew 7:17: "So every good tree bears good fruit,
but the bad trees bear bad fruit."

T he next morning I awake with a renewed vigor.

I can't wait to tackle the next 50 yards with The Fisherman.

When I meet him at the pier he greets me with a sly smile. "I was watching a baseball game on TV last night," The Fisherman says. "This dude hit a walk-off home run to win the game. As he crossed home plate his teammates swarmed him and they all did this funky jive."

"I saw the same game," I tell The Fisherman, revealing to him my life-long love of the New York Yankees.

"It reminded me of one of those crazy touchdown dances football players do these days," he says, shaking his head.

I just stand there, staring, mouth wide open.

"But what would an old guy like me know about one of them?" The Fisherman says, bending over in laughter.

How did he know…

He lets his laughter roll for a few minutes, unwrapping an egg sandwich in the process, and manages a few bites between fits of giggles.

"Let me tell you something," The Fisherman says, pouring some coffee from his thermos, his laughter finally subsiding. "You know those five traits we talked about?"

"Judgment, Unselfishness, Initiative, Courage, Endurance?" I quickly rattle off.

"That's right," The Fisherman says, as he puts down his coffee and looks me in the eye. "Lead with those five traits, and great things will happen. Follow the next five traits, and you'll set yourself apart from all others."

I am ready to run through a brick wall for this guy.

The Fisherman tells me the next trait: Bearing.

A smile lights up my face. This is right down my alley. I'm the head coach of the Missouri State Bears. We're in the process of creating an entire new culture: Bear Up!

To embrace a new culture you need other great leaders to help you install a winning philosophy. As my friend Jon Gordon always told me, "culture is always dynamic."

So I hire men who are smart, hard-working and genuine people. I always believe these qualities in a person produce great results.

Those men included: Sean Coughlin, Mack Brown, Justin Kramer and Trent Figg. Mario Verduzco, Jason Ray, Lanear Sampson and Jake Morse, Stephen Bravo-Brown and Marty Spieler on offense. (Some coaches who did a great job moved on to other opportunities.) On defense we hired Marcus Yokeley, Chris Morton, Munir Prince and Kenji Jackson. Just like the offensive guys Peter Badovinac, Jerone (Juice) Williams and Adam Gristick moved on to other opportunities. The last and most critical hire, was Adam Lang our strength and conditioning coach.

The important point is to hire good people and let them build things together on a daily basis, because…

"Bearing is how you handle yourself, how you carry yourself, your poise," The Fisherman says, "The bearing of a champion."

He whips his fishing line into the ocean with the grace of a painter.

"It begins with the mind," The Fisherman says, a determined look in his eyes. "Take Muhammad Ali, for instance. He thought he was the best before he was the best. You live your thoughts, and to be a great leader you must use your thoughts to empower your team and coaches.

"What you think, you become."

The Fisherman goes on to cite several studies about the power of positive thinking. One such study centered on people whose anxiety disorders sow thoughts of negativity. Participants were asked to replace those negative thoughts with possible positive outcomes.

Researchers found that, a month later, all groups reported significantly reduced anxiety and worry. More surprisingly, even unrelated positive thinking can counter worry.

"The mind," The Fisherman says, "is the best player on the field."

As I walk home that morning I think about being a young coach again and the head coaches who have influenced me. Most notably Ed Sweeney, who always said "Act like you're a champion," and Gary Pinkel, who always said, "Act like you have been there before."

I realize your thoughts and actions must be such that you would want others to model. This doesn't mean perfection, but it does mean doing things the right way.

BEARING

Know:

Bearing is how you conduct and carry yourself. Your manners should reflect alertness, competence, confidence and competitiveness through emotional control.

Improvements:

Hold yourself to the highest standard. Never be content with the minimum.

CHAPTER TWELVE

Accountability

First Corinthians 4:2: "In this case moreover, it is required of stewards that one be found trustworthy and accountable."

Walking the beach the next day I feel a different strut in my steps.

To be a leader The Fisherman is saying, in my eyes, "If you act like a leader and dream like a leader you can be a leader."

Sounds easy enough.

I think about these character traits until I come upon The Fisherman.

"Morning!" I say to my new friend.

"Back at ya," he says, his line already in the ocean's depths.

"I gotta tell ya, what you said yesterday really resonated with me," I say, tapping on the pier's railing. "I'm ready to step up my game with acting like a leader."

The Fisherman bends down and slowly lowers his fishing rod until it's resting on the pier, stands up and stares me straight in the eyes.

I've seen this look before.

"Act?" he says, his eyes narrowing. "Stec, you can't *act* like a leader. People want leaders who are accountable, not people who merely act like it. People believe in leaders they can trust. Show people they can count on you, and they will trust you.

"It's about one word, accountability."

I open my mouth to speak, but he beats me to the punch.

"We're both baseball fans, right?" The Fisherman says while picking up his rod and slowly reeling in the line.

"Yes, sir."

"Ever hear of an umpire by the name of Jim Joyce?"

"No, sir."

The Fisherman goes on to explain the story of Jim Joyce, the Major League Baseball umpire who was a field umpire when Armando Galarraga was pitching a perfect game. The top of the ninth inning came. First out is a fly ball. The second is a ground-out. Routine stuff. On the next batter Galarraga is running to cover first base after a slow ground ball. The third out, and a perfect game, are only a few feet away. Joyce moves in to make the call. He signals the runner safe.

The perfect game is over.

Shortly after the game ends Joyce is running to the dugout and hears people screaming that he blew the call, that the runner he called safe was actually out. After watching the replay in the locker room, Joyce realizes he's made the biggest mistake of his life. The runner was out.

His heart sinks.

Instead of running and ducking, Joyce allows media access to the umpires' locker room—a rarity. He takes full responsibility for missing the call. After the media leave, Joyce asks an official if he can talk to Galarraga. When the two men meet in the bowels of the stadium, they embrace, and while hugging Galarraga tells Joyce, "We are all human." Through tears Joyce apologizes in English and Spanish.

At his next game, Joyce was the home plate umpire, and when it was time to exchange line-up cards Galarraga emerged from the dugout. The crowd stood and erupted in cheers. The moment was caught on television and broadcast across the country. Millions saw it. That's how Jim Joyce and Armando Galarraga are remembered—not for a blown call, but for a display of sportsmanship and affection that transcended what happened on the ball field.

"We are all human," The Fisherman says. "Imagine if Jim Joyce hadn't owned up to his mistake, if he hadn't been accountable for his actions. He never would have had that amazing exchange with that young pitcher, and their reunion at the plate the next game would have never happened.

"That's the power of being accountable."

The Fisherman stops reeling in his line and looks at me again.

"Coach, can you be trusted? Can your men count on you?"

The question stops me cold. I have never asked myself if the players and coaches could trust me, if they knew they can count on me, to always be there for them. The Fisherman made me realize accountability entails both of those qualities.

My thoughts go quickly to our Insight Bowl game against the University of Iowa. After a tough loss, we were driving to the airport the next morning. You see, we threw an interception with 1:56 on the clock that Iowa ran back for a pick six to win the game. We were in field goal range and should have run the football to run time off the clock. Coach Pinkel looked at me and said, "Can you believe we threw that pick?" Looking back, I asked why the offensive coordinator called a pass.

Without hesitation coach said, "I called that play!" I knew he didn't, but he had the back of his coach. Talk about accountability. Talk about trusting a man to protect his team.

As I walk home I feel the weight of the world on my shoulders. The Fisherman's statement rings in my ears, "Can your men count on you?" As I think things through, I realize it's not just me, but more importantly, my family.

The game of football and life always pulls you in many different directions. You must make sure leadership starts at home, and you must be accountable to your family. In my case, I have an awesome wife, MaryBeth, and an incredible daughter, Amanda.

As a coach you are always recruiting and looking for players that have great physical ability. However, The Fisherman taught me the greatest ability to have is accountability.

ACCOUNTABILITY

Know:

Accountability is your performance of all duties. It means you can be trusted to do your job. Your willingness to support the team plan and the chain of command. It is putting your BEST effort forward to achieve at the highest level.

Improvements:

Create habits of being where you're supposed to be on time. Make NO EXCUSES and carry out your tasks to the best of your ability, while also holding your teammates to the same standard.

CHAPTER THIRTEEN

Integrity

Psalm 41:12: "Because of my integrity you upheld me and set me in your presence forever."

My focus is razor sharp the next morning. The Fisherman's lessons are seeping through my thick skull.

The weight I felt on my shoulders yesterday is replaced with an airy confidence. I have a bounce to my step, even through sand. Sometimes you just need to learn how to lead yourself. The Fisherman is the ultimate guide.

As I approach the pier, I see the old man take a long pull on his rod while leaning back, one foot behind the other, his rod almost in an arc, and then quickly reel in his line. He repeats this process until a fish emerges from the water and flops onto the pier.

I run up to congratulate The Fisherman, and I realize I'm way more excited than he is.

The old man methodically removes the hook from the fish's mouth, the head of the baited shrimp the only thing left on the hook.

"Red drum," he says while holding the fish gently in his hands as if it were a newborn baby.

"How do you know?"

"See that red color on the top?" The Fisherman says, pointing out the obvious.

"Sure do," I say, feigning my fishing prowess.

"The red fades into a white underbelly, but the telltale sign is that one big black spot on its tail. It's a juvenile."

I watch as The Fisherman places his catch in a large bucket of water and walks toward the stairs of the pier.

"Too young to keep," he says over his shoulder, answering the question percolating in my mind.

As I watch him descend the stairs I wonder who The Fisherman really is. What experiences has he lived through? What has he seen?

Lost in thought I don't notice that he's returned and is placing another fresh shrimp on his hook.

"Caught a lot bigger ones than that," the old man says, and then, without prompting, recounts several fishing tales from his past, from places all over the world. Hawaii in the central Pacific Ocean. East China Sea off Japan. Catching countless Muskie in North Carolina's New River.

It's a lot to take in, and hard to believe. I call The Fisherman out on one of his stories, and he gives me the look I've come to dread.

"God's honest truth," he says, making me feel as small as that shrimp on the end of his hook.

I must have ignited something in The Fisherman.

"One of the greatest qualities is the ability to tell the truth," he says. "Did you know studies have shown that people lie approximately 1.65 times a day? You should read the article written by Gad Saad: "The Pinocchio Effect: Lying in Daily Life."

I've been told I have a Bob Hope nose but never thought about Pinocchio's.

"People don't always want to hear the truth, but they respect you more for being honest with them, instead of placating them," The Fisherman says, casting his line into the ocean. "Think back to our talk on courage. Do the right thing. Living with integrity is the right thing."

The Fisherman leaves me a lot to think about as I walk back

to the house. He just called me out on the way I am living my life, while at the same time I was thinking his stories were exaggerated or not even true.

I flash back to my childhood and remember lying to my father. You know, the "little white lie."

My good buddy Bruce Grim (God rest his soul) and I pulled off the neighbor's distributer cap for a joke; seems like this particular guy was the butt of a lot of them. Obviously the car couldn't start and we didn't know that the spark plugs went back in a certain order. Once they found out it was us, we of course tried to lie our way out of it. I got the pummeling of my life from my dad. I'll never forget what he said. "Just remember, when you lie you better remember what you say!"

I realized at that moment I wasn't smart enough to remember. Plus, it's easier to live with the truth.

INTEGRITY

Know:

Having integrity means you are honest and truthful with what you say and do. You make honesty, sense of duty (responsibility) and sound moral principles above all else.

Improvements:

Be honest and truthful at all times. Stand up for what is right NOT wrong.

CHAPTER FOURTEEN

Loyalty

Proverbs 3:3: "Never let go of loyalty and faithfulness. Tie them around your neck, write them on your heart."

A dream comes to me in the dark of night.

It's like the dream from several nights ago, the one in which I watch a company of all-black recruits drill with precision in a driving rain.

My eyes meet the drill instructor's, just like the last dream. A flash of lightning illuminates the Marines eagle, globe and anchor on his hat and the words Montford Point Marines. It's like I'm watching a movie for the second time.

In this dream the drill instructor stops in front of me. His company keeps marching.

He turns and stares right at me, the pelting rain doing nothing to interrupt his gaze.

I've seen this look before. The Fisherman?

"Coach Stec!" the drill instructor barks.

I try to utter a response, but my voice is barely audible.

"You are the sculptor of young men's minds. Do not buckle under the weight of this responsibility. Follow the path The Fisherman has set before you."

The drill instructor bends down and scoops up a handful of mud. With his thumb he smears the mud over my eyes.

"When you awake," he says, "you'll see things differently."

I wake up rubbing my eyes, the morning light a stinging blur separating sleepy drowsiness from the enthusiasm for a new day.

A renewed purpose bolts me out of bed.

I practically run to the pier to meet The Fisherman. The dream is still vividly replaying in my mind.

"Were you a drill instructor in a past life?" I ask The Fisherman, practically out of breath.

The Fisherman laughs.

"Nah, not quite. I was a corporal, just went about my business."

The Fisherman casts his line into the ocean.

"I need to apologize for yesterday," I say, staring down at the pier.

"Apology accepted,"The Fisherman says. "Not needed. But accepted."

I muster the courage to ask the old man a question.

"What was it like for you in boot camp?"

The Fisherman stares out at his line. In the distance a squadron of pelicans effortlessly cuts through the sky southward. The Fisherman and the pelicans seek something they cannot see but they trust is there. Faith is required of all beings, especially during the toughest of days.

The Fisherman knows all about faith. And despair. And resilience.

He also knows his history, and I'm an eager listener, hanging on every word.

President Franklin D. Roosevelt ordered all armed services to admit black recruits in 1942.

Racial discrimination banned black recruits from the Marine Corps' training facilities at Parris Island, South Carolina, and San Diego, during the course of World War II, and some years after. Their destination would be a segregated boot camp in Montford Point, North Carolina, where roughly 20,000 recruits passed through the camp between 1942 and the facility's closing in 1949.

The old man explains how railroad tracks divided white residents in nearby Jacksonville, North Carolina, from the hastily constructed boot camp at Montford Point.

Hostility toward the black recruits, who began arriving in the summer of 1942, was intense. They couldn't go into Jacksonville for a bite to eat. Restaurants, transportation, bathrooms—all segregated. They couldn't even go to the main base at nearby Camp Lejeune, where whites were allowed.

They were second-class citizens.

Major Gen. Thomas Holcomb, the top-ranking Marine in 1941, had this to say, "If it were a question of having a Marine Corps of 5,000 whites or 250,000 Negroes, I would rather have the whites."

Still, they were willing to fight, and die, for their country. They felt loyalty for each other and the United States.

Montford Point recruits saw action in War War II's most profound battles, including Iwo Jima and Saipan. While not having reached the prestige of other trailblazers, like the Tuskegee Airmen, the Montford Point Marines are credited for playing a crucial role in integrating the Marine Corps.

The Fisherman was on the frontlines of history.

"It's about loyalty to a cause, loyalty to a belief that in your soul you know is right," The Fisherman says. "Having honor in the plan and executing the plan. Once people, or in your case, players, trust the plan and are committed to the plan, success will follow."

Loyalty is the most powerful ally in the fight against injustice, the old man goes on to explain. It was the glue that held him and all of his fellow recruits together when the world was against them, their dreams almost drowned in the infernal marshland of the North Carolina coast. And it was the mantle on which they fought and died in unforgiving hellholes like Saipan and Iwo Jima.

"Without loyalty," he says, "you might as well pack your bags."

The Fisherman reviews all the lessons he's shared with me on the pier. He explains how when you truly grasp the meaning of each quality, you ultimately gain the loyalty of others.

"You see, loyalty isn't a word … it's a lifestyle."

To build loyalty The Fisherman offers three important questions.

-Can I trust you?

-Are you committed?

-Do you care?

"Once these elements are evident," The Fisherman says, "loyalty within any organization will always exist."

I thank The Fisherman for his sacrifice and leave the pier.

After walking for a while I sit and stare out at the ocean.

I think about all the successful teams I have been blessed to be a part of. These teams had something in common, loyalty was not just talked about—it was exhibited.

Thinking back to the tough times during a season, it was the trust and commitment the coaches and players had for each other that saw us through. Some would say we loved each other. For families, teams and organizations to be truly successful they must be loyal to one another, and through loyalty, love is evident.

I reminisce about my career path. I left the University of Toledo and Gary Pinkel to go to Rutgers University. It was a time in my life where I wanted to climb the ladder of success to more money and a bigger program, a higher division.

As it turned out, the head coach and the entire staff were fired after five unsuccessful seasons. However, as fate and strong prayers intervened, Gary Pinkel got the University of Missouri job and hired us back. Coach showed his loyalty to me and my family.

To quote the great Paul Harvey, "Now for the rest of the story…" My wife and I were offered an NFL job two weeks after Coach Pinkel hired us. Talk about testing someone's loyalty! We stayed with our decision to go to Missouri, and fourteen years later our loyalty was rewarded with a great life for our family, the love of a great coaching staff, and most importantly, many great, lifelong relationships with our players. We were fortunate in that time to be blessed with much success.

The Fisherman is right—loyalty is easily attainable when you understand the other qualities of leadership.

LOYALTY

Know:

You are loyal when you are devoted to your school, team and all members of the organization. Unwavering loyalty to ALL people up and down the chain of command.

Improvements:

Never discuss issues with people not within your organization. Never talk about your coaches (or) teammates unfavorably in front of others. All conflicts should be behind closed doors. Once decisions are made, carry out all assignments with knowledge as if it were your idea.

CHAPTER FIFTEEN
Enthusiasm

Colossians 3:23: "Whatever you do, work at it enthusiastically
with all of your heart, as working for the Lord."

My steps through the sand are extra heavy this morning. Usually I'm relaxed and reenergized toward the end of vacation, but this time it's different. I realize my talks with The Fisherman are coming to an end, leaving me feeling glum.

Will I have the courage to see his lessons through on my own?

The Fisherman senses the weight on my mind as I approach our usual meeting place.

"I could spot your gloominess from a mile away," The Fisherman says between sips of coffee. "Coach, body language is the number one language in the world, and every single person speaks it."

I share with him my thoughts of having to leave the beach and get back to work.

The Fisherman lets out a little chuckle as he puts down his coffee and pulls a mud minnow out of a small bucket, and begins baiting his J-hook.

"People were designed to work, starting with Adam and Eve, who were put in the garden to work, to current times, the need to work to support your family," he says. "Work is what sustains human beings."

Instead of being downcast like me, The Fisherman is his usual upbeat self. He is excited and enthusiastic about my leaving the beach.

I am taken aback by his reaction, especially since I am so disappointed to be going.

His enthusiasm, The Fisherman explains, is for the thought of me using our talks with my team. He drives home the point that the most important quality as a leader is to show, have and display enthusiasm for every task you encounter.

The Fisherman quotes Ralph Waldo Emerson:

"Enthusiasm is one of the most powerful engines of success. When you do a thing, do it with all your might. Put your whole soul into it. Stamp it with your own personality. Be active, be energetic, be enthusiastic and faithful, and you will accomplish your objective. Nothing great was ever achieved without enthusiasm."

"Most people just use the last sentence of Emerson's quote," The Fisherman says. "But the first part is what's most important."

Knowing that this is my last chance to soak up The Fisherman's wisdom I ask if I may sit for a while.

"Sure," The Fisherman says, as he reaches over to switch on his portable radio. A familiar song fills the ether as the morning mist starts to give way to a lazy sun, lifting my mood. Again, it's The Boss singing "Thunder Road." Concentrating on the words, I really feel the song is speaking directly to me.

After I arrive back at the beach house, I look up the Emerson quote to understand it better, and I realize The Fisherman is right.

You can be a great leader by showing your love, passion and, yes, enthusiasm for your family, coaches and, more importantly, your players.

Your players, coaches and the people you encounter will be the next leaders. Encourage them to do just that—lead with enthusiasm.

I think about enthusiasm, and I am reminded of a young high school quarterback I recruited out of South Lake Carroll High School in Texas, Chase Daniel. Chase came off the bench as a true freshman in the fourth quarter to replace our injured starting quarterback, Brad Smith. Brad Smith was a phenomenal player for Missouri, who went on to play more than ten years in the NFL. The game Chase was called in for was against Iowa State. Missouri was down by 14 in the fourth quarter and Chase went in and led the team to an overtime win, which gave the team a bowl bid to the Independence Bowl. Chase always said, "Be an encourager, not a discourager."

It is amazing how you can learn the smallest of things from anybody in your organization. Chase is now starting his tenth year in the NFL. I look back and think, he was a great player, but more importantly he is an enthusiastic leader.

Remember what Emerson said. Enthusiasm is one of the most powerful engines of success.

ENTHUSIASM

Know:

To be enthusiastic, practice sincere interest, excitement and energy in the performance of all tasks. This will make you optimistic, cheerful and willing to accept challenges.

Improvements:

Understanding and belief in the plan will add to your enthusiasm for work. Understand all jobs must get done for success.

CHAPTER SIXTEEN

The Fisherman

It is here. Departure day from the beach.

I have an overwhelming sense of peace. I feel like I've downloaded a lifetime of wisdom from The Fisherman in just one short week.

I think back to the first day I met him, of walking toward that pier.

How I trudged through the sand preoccupied with "Xs" and "Os" as I plotted the next game plan, unaware of the beautiful painting in front of me, the sun melting into the ocean, shrouding the beach in a haze of cranberry and purple. How can I visualize that scene now even though I was unaware then?

Something greater is at work in all of us.

I help my wife and daughter pack the car for the drive home.

"Allow me," someone says, taking a suitcase from my wife's hands and placing it in our SUV.

"Thank you," my wife says.

"For what?" I say, catching only that part of the conversation. I look toward the back of the car, only to see a familiar face smiling back at me.

"What brings you away from your fishing hole?" I say to The Fisherman, jutting out my hand to shake his, a broad smile crossing my face.

"Just thought I'd do what you've been doing every morning and go for a little stroll," The Fisherman says, returning my smile.

I start to introduce The Fisherman to my wife and daughter when I realize I have no idea what his real name is.

Sensing my awkwardness The Fisherman removes his Montford Point Marine Association hat and extends his hand. "Juice Baile," he says. "I've heard so much about the both of you. It's a pleasure to meet you."

"This is the guy I've been talking to every day on my walks," I tell my wife and daughter, his real name already beginning to fade from my memory.

"So you do exist," my wife says, flashing a knowing glance my way.

"Yes ma'am, here I am, right here in the flesh," The Fisherman says.

We make small talk for a few minutes before The Fisherman turns to look me in the eyes—the way he did so many times during our talks on the pier—and imparts one last nugget of knowledge.

"Remember as you walk on your new journey of leadership, true leadership begins by example, not by perfection."

With that he bids goodbye to the three of us, places his cap on his head, and walks toward the ocean. I go back to the task of loading the SUV.

A small mist begins to fall. After a few minutes I turn around for one last glance at The Fisherman but he is nowhere to be found.

Several hours into the drive my thoughts wander back to my talks with The Fisherman. As Interstate 40 twists through the Great Smoky Mountains I'm reminded of how small all of us truly are—that all our worries and fears are of our own making. That we're part of something much bigger.

I begin to zero in on this morning packing the car when The Fisherman appeared out of nowhere. How he introduced himself to my wife and daughter.

"Juice Baile."

I keep repeating the name in my head, and the lessons delivered by The Fisherman, while tapping the steering wheel with each word: Juice. Baile. Juice. Baile

Then it strikes me: Each quality of leadership begins with the letters of his name:

Judgment

Unselfishness

Initiative

Courage

Endurance

Bearing

Accountability

Integrity

Loyalty

Enthusiasm

I want to blurt it out. Juice Baile! How could I miss something so obvious?

My wife is fast asleep next to me. I look in the rearview mirror and my daughter is also asleep.

I think back to our very first meeting. How he was walking down the steps of the pier. The movie replays in my mind.

"Stec," I say, jutting out my hand.

"They call me The Fisherman," he says, gripping my hand with a strength that jars me back to reality.

"What kind of name is The Fisherman?"

"What kind of name is Stec?"

I like him from the start.

Smiling, content in knowing that something unexplainable has given my life a new purpose, I switch on my iPod connected to the SUV's stereo. A familiar song fills the silence. "No Surrender" comes alive in the car. Noticing the unbelievable coincidence, I realize as a leader you can't retreat or surrender from the unmistakable qualities that The Fisherman has taught me.

Emerging from the mountains the highway begins to straighten out. The sun is setting, shrouding the road in a haze of cranberry and purple.

Just like that morning on the beach when I met The Fisherman. This time I notice.

Matthew 4:19: "And he said to them, Follow me and I will make you Fishers of men."

- the end -